POPPY DAY

Eliza Berison

First worldwide publication in Great Britain in 2022
by DDR Publishing UK.

This edition published 2022 by DDR Publishing UK.
ISBN: 978-1-915146-10-6

Edited by Dan Berison

Printed in Great Britain.

This book belongs to

....

POPPY DAY

Eliza Berison

November
11th
(Silence at 11am)
always need milk.

Today is a special day,
one always to remember,

where we think of the past,
and one distant November.

Mum turns on the radio,
a poppy close to her heart.

For Big Ben we are waiting,
it's nearly time to start!

I place a poppy on my chest,
Mum gives me a hand.

She talks of valiant soldiers,
heroic on the land.

Remember those daring pilots,
soaring way up high,

that battled so fiercely,
darting through the sky!

Remember all those sailors,
daring the deep blue sea.

Lionhearted warriors,
they travelled so bravely.

Eleven rings out
and we hear the radio chime.

Time to be silent,
honour heroes through time.

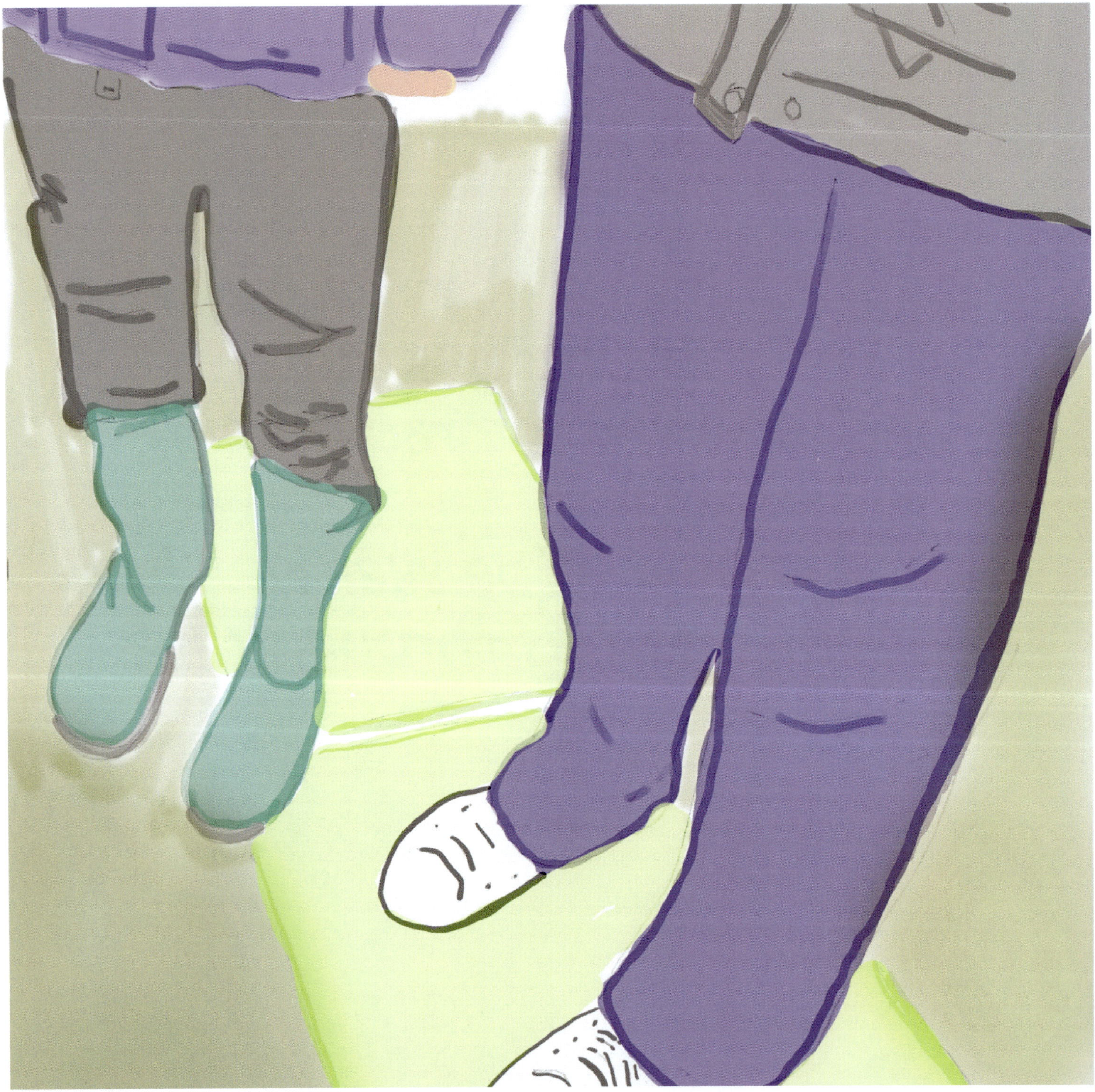

I try not to shuffle,
to stand so quietly.

I feel so proud wearing
my beautiful poppy.

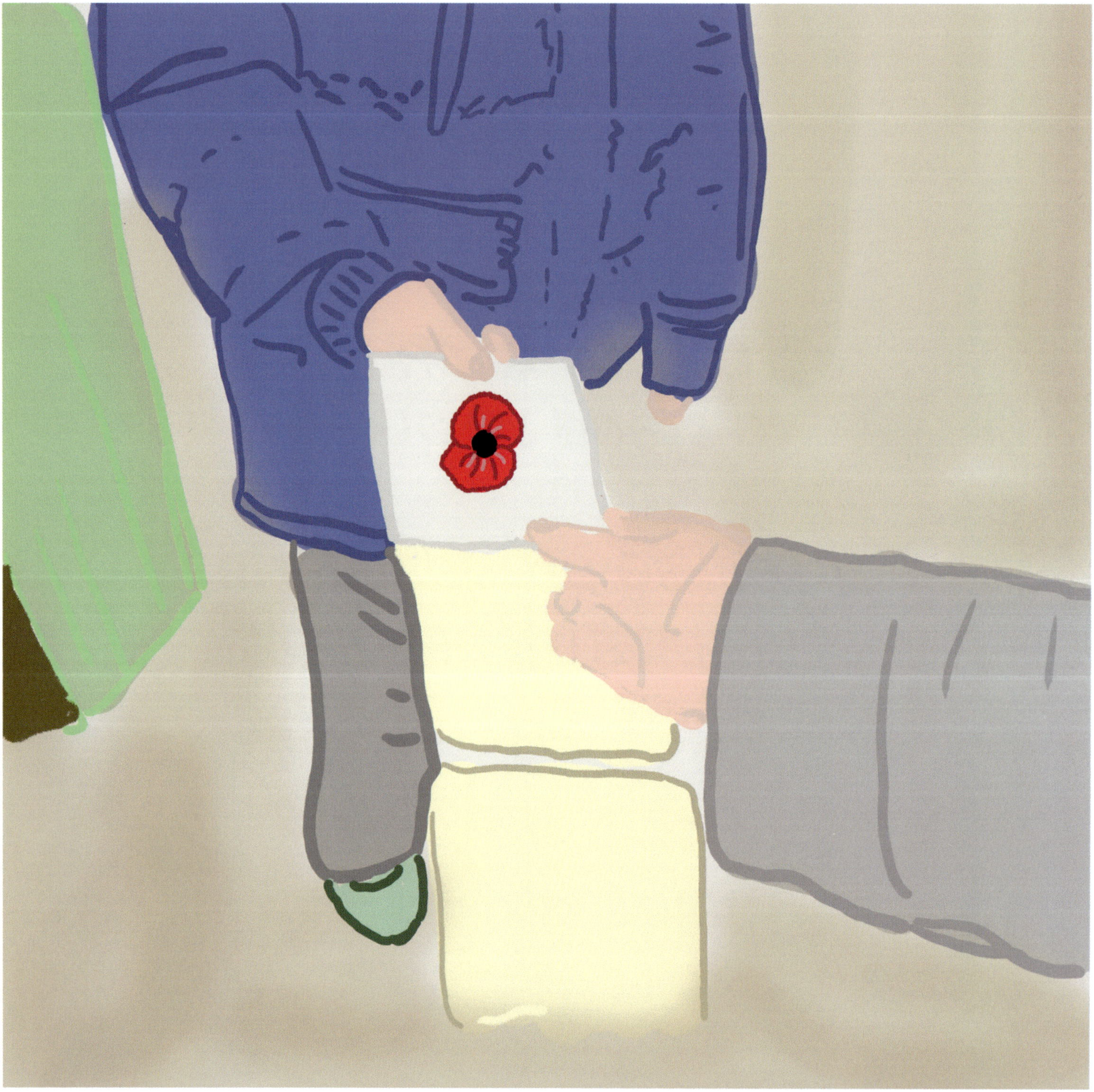

Two minutes later,
the trumpet makes such a racket,

but this day isn't over yet,
as Mum hands me a packet.

Let these seeds be a reminder,
planted deep in the ground.

Give them plenty of sun
and water all year round!

I place each seed down
and pack them with mud.

I drop a little water on
as Mum said I should.

Winter comes and goes
and spring quickly arrives,

the garden's so vibrant,
my poppies are so alive!

I lean down and whisper,
to my poppy, so red!

I'm glad you grew so big
and strong,
in my flower bed.

Today is a special day,
one always to remember,

where we think of the past,
and one distant November.

Dedicated to all the valiant, fierce, lionhearted heroes.

We will always remember and never forget.

Make a poppy with your fingers and thumb

1. Press down with thumb

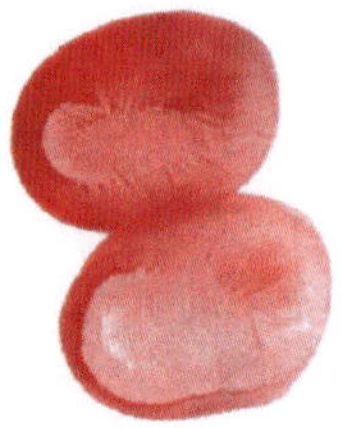

2. Press again with thumb

3. Dot the black with your finger

4. Paint your finger green and angle it across the page.

YOU JUST PAINTED A POPPY!

WHY NOT TURN IT INTO A SCENE?

Printed in Great Britain
by Amazon

10496228R00020